Grace
Meets Grit

A 30-day Devotional
for
Women Who Ride

Kimberly Lonngren

Publishing

To The Women Who Ride

This devotional journal is dedicated to all the women who ride. The strength it takes to be Christian and to be a part of the motorcycle lifestyle takes dedication. We will explore the themes of freedom, faith, and the challenges of life, all within the context of a motorcycle rider's experience. It is written to encourage a balance to both the physical and spiritual life of those who love to ride. As we embark on our journeys, the open road stretches before us, full of promise and possibility. Just as the road winds and turns, so too does our spiritual path. Let us invite God to search the depths of our hearts, to know our anxieties, and to guide our steps. Use this devotional through the next 30 days to grow closer to God and understand your heart while finding grace for yourself and your experiences.

There is a scripture for every fear, heartache, and crossroads you may face. Use this devotional to find scripture that touches your heart and take it with you as you ride the curves of life.

What anxieties or fears might be holding you back from fully experiencing the open road both physically and spiritually?

Psalms 139:24 "Search me, O God, and know my heart; test me and know my anxious thoughts."

Each day is a new day for reflection. This 30-day devotional is set up with busy women in mind and will be touching on a wide variety of topics and themes, from self-esteem and relationships to finding God's love and grace. Each day offers a moment of reflection and guidance and reminds each woman who reads this that you have the strength to take on whatever may come your way.

Because of God's love for the Israelites, he noted how they felt. He also understood they had worn these heavy garments for an exceptionally long time. He made a promise to exchange those heavy garments for new lighter ones. Garments of praise. Garments of joy. Beauty for ashes. As we receive that gift, Jesus exchanges our hurts for joy. Our critical spirit for hope. Our overwhelmed soul for rest. Sometimes that is instant, sometimes it takes more time, and we feel relief may never come but the good news is that through faith and prayer, miracles happen every day! God wants us to talk to him, he wants us to share our fears and frustrations with him and with others

With Peace and Blessings,

Kimberly

DAY 1 *Scripture*

> *Enter through the narrow gate*
> *for wide is the gate and broad is*
> *a road that leads to destruction,*
> *and many enter through it but*
> *small is the gate and narrow is*
> *the road that leads to life and*
> *only a few find it.*
> *Matthew 7:13-14*

The Open Road and The Narrow Gate

To anyone who has had the joy of riding a motorcycle, you know the allure of the open road, and how it beckons us with its promise of adventure. It's a place where worries fade, where the present moment is all that matters. We feel a sense of power and control navigating the curves and conquering challenges and this freedom can be intoxicating. We can easily get caught up in the thrill of the ride in the pursuit of speed and excitement and neglect the spiritual side of the journey.

With its freedom also comes the feel of wind in our hair, the miles stretching before us, the smells of fresh cut grass or honeysuckles. It gives us the freedom to see for miles with no obstruction, but we know around every curve or over a big hill there are dangers on the road and so are there dangers in life. The Bible speaks of a narrow gate, a path to righteousness that can be challenging to follow. It can be hard being a woman and even harder being a woman who rides. As riders, we crave that sense of liberation, the feeling of escaping the constraints of everyday life but true freedom, the kind that truly satisfies, isn't just about the open road. It's about finding freedom in Christ.

Reflection: On your next ride remember to seek both the freedom of the open road and the freedom found in Christ. May your journey be filled with joy, adventure, and a deep sense of peace.

Prayer:
Heavenly Father, as I prepare to embark on this journey I place my trust in your loving hands.

Guide my hands and feet, keep my mind alert and focused, and protect me from harm. May the wind in my hair be a reminder of your constant presence, and the open road a symbol of the endless possibilities that await.

Grant me courage and wisdom on this ride, and may my spirit be uplifted by your grace.

Amen.

DATE

S   M   T   W   T   F   S

TAKE A MOMENT EACH DAY TO REFLECT ON THE THINGS
YOU'RE THANKFUL FOR

TODAY'S FOCUS

_____
_____
_____

TODAY I AM GRATEFUL FOR...

_____
_____
_____

SOMETHING THAT INSPIRED ME TODAY

PEOPLE I'M GRATEFUL TO HAVE
IN MY LIFE

Answered prayers

_____
_____
_____
_____
_____
_____

Notes & Free Thoughts

_____

_____

_____

_____

_____

_____

_____

_____

_____

_____

_____

_____

_____

_____

_____

_____

_____

_____

DAY 2 *scripture*

> *Have I not commanded you to be strong and courageous do not be afraid do not be discouraged for the Lord your God will be with you wherever you go.*
>
> *Joshua 1:9*

A Life of Adventure

Do you remember the first time you were on a motorcycle? For most of us we remember every detail. The emotions often are a mix of fear and exhilaration. Just like in Joshua, we needed courage to get through the nervousness. We needed strength to keep going. Maybe your heart was pounding in your chest, your palms sweaty. The bike was rumbling beneath you, and even though your body was still, your mind was racing with "What if's?" What if I stall out? What if I lean too far? What if I can't stop in time?

Maybe you did stall out. Maybe you did brake too hard and lurched forward with a jolt that rattled your confidence. Maybe you took a curve unsure of how to lean, unsure of how to trust. But even then, something inside you told you to try again. To push past the fear. To keep going. There was something wild and freeing about the wind in your face and the hum of the engine—a whisper of freedom that tugged at your soul.

At first, many of us weren't even in control, we sat behind someone else. A father, husband, sister, or friend. We had to trust. We had to release our grip on control, lean into the turns, and learn how to enjoy the ride.

It was scary, but it was also the start of something beautiful: the beginning of a new adventure.

Our spiritual lives aren't very different. God calls us to a journey that isn't always smooth or predictable. There are times we'll stall, lose our balance, or hit the brakes too hard. But just like that first ride, we're not alone. God is with us in every twist and turn. He doesn't promise an easy road, but He does promise His presence —and that makes all the difference.

When we surrender the handlebars of our life and allow God to lead, fear gives way to trust, and panic is replaced with peace. He knows the road ahead. He knows how fast we need to go, when to slow down, and when to lean into the curve.

So take a breath. Let go of fear. Be strong and courageous. Whether your road is straight or winding, smooth or bumpy, God is with you—wherever you go.

Reflection: How do you embrace the spirit of adventure that comes with riding? Is it by exploring new roads, discovering hidden gems, or stepping outside your comfort zone? Whatever it is for you, remember that God is with you on every journey!

Prayer: Heavenly Father, as I embark on this journey, both on two wheels and in life, I ask for your guidance and blessing.

Grant me the courage to embrace the unknown, to explore new horizons, and to chase my dreams with passion and determination.

May I find adventure not just on the open road, but also in the depths of my own soul.

May I encounter kindness and beauty on my travels, and may I be a source of light and inspiration to others. Protect me from harm and fill my heart with a sense of wonder and awe.

Amen

DATE

S   M   T   W   T   F   S

TAKE A MOMENT EACH DAY TO REFLECT ON THE THINGS YOU'RE THANKFUL FOR

TODAY'S FOCUS

_____
_____
_____

TODAY I AM GRATEFUL FOR...

_____
_____
_____

| SOMETHING THAT INSPIRED ME TODAY | PEOPLE I'M GRATEFUL TO HAVE IN MY LIFE |

Answered prayers

_____
_____
_____
_____
_____
_____

Notes & Free Thoughts

_____

_____

_____

_____

_____

_____

_____

_____

_____

_____

_____

_____

_____

_____

_____

_____

_____

♥

DAY 3 *scripture*

> "Don't be deceived, my dear brothers and sisters. Every good and perfect gift is from above, coming down from the Father of the heavenly lights, who does not change like shifting shadows.
> James 1:16-17"

Navigating Curves

We all know the thrill of leaning into a curve on a motorcycle. The bike responds, the world tilts, and for a moment, we are one with the machine and the road. But life, like a winding road, is full of unexpected curves. Some are gentle, easily navigated. Others are sharp, challenging our skill and our nerves. James reminds us, amidst these twists and turns, of a constant truth: every good and perfect gift comes from above.

As women riders, we understand the vulnerability of the open road. We know that things can change quickly, shadows can shift, and unexpected obstacles can appear in our path. Just as we lean into a curve, trusting our training and our bikes, we must also lean into our trusting in the unchanging nature of God.

James tells us not to be deceived. The world may try to convince us that we are alone in navigating these curves, that our strength is solely our own. But true strength comes from the Father, the source of every good and perfect gift. He is the consistent in our lives, the one who does not change like shifting shadows.

Reflection: What curves have you encountered recently, both on the road and in life? How has your faith helped you navigate these challenges? How can you cultivate a stronger reliance on God during difficult times?

Prayer: Heavenly Father, thank you for the gift of riding and for your constant presence in my life. Help me to trust in you as I navigate the curves of the road and the curves of life.

Remind me that you are the source of all strength and wisdom, and that you never change.

Amen

DATE

S   M   T   W   T   F   S

TAKE A MOMENT EACH DAY TO REFLECT ON THE THINGS YOU'RE THANKFUL FOR

TODAY'S FOCUS

_____

_____

_____

TODAY I AM GRATEFUL FOR...

_____

_____

_____

SOMETHING THAT INSPIRED ME TODAY

PEOPLE I'M GRATEFUL TO HAVE IN MY LIFE

Answered prayers

_____

_____

_____

_____

_____

_____

Notes & Free Thoughts

_____

_____

_____

_____

_____

_____

_____

_____

_____

_____

_____

_____

_____

_____

_____

_____

_____

_____

_____

_____

_____

DAY 4 *scripture*

"

This is the day the Lord has made; let us rejoice and be glad in it.

Psalms 118:24

"

Living in the present moment

The hum of the engine, the feel of the road beneath the tires, the wind whispering past your helmet- these are the sensations that draw us to the open road. On a motorcycle, we are intensely present. The focus required for safe riding demands our full attention, pushing aside the worries of yesterday and the anxieties of tomorrow. It is in these moments, immersed in the present, that we can truly experience the joy of riding.

Psalms 118:24 is a simple yet powerful verse urging us to embrace the present moment, to find joy and gratitude in the here and now. How often do we let our minds wander during the ride rehashing past mistakes or fretting about future obligations? If we did, we would miss the beauty of the passing landscape, the camaraderie of fellow riders, and the sheer exhilaration of the ride itself.

As women we often juggle multiple roles: mother, wife, daughter, sister, friend, professional. When our minds are a whirlwind of to-dos and what if's, riding can be a sanctuary, a place where we can escape the mental clutter and simply *be*, it's an opportunity to connect with ourselves, with nature, and with God.

Cultivating presence takes practice just as we hone

our riding skills, we must also train our minds to stay focused on the present mindfulness techniques such as deep breathing and focusing on sensory input can help us anchor ourselves in the now.

Reflection: This week make a conscious effort to be present, to feel the rumble of the engine, the grip of the tires, the warmth of the sun on your skin. Notice the details of the world around you, the colors, the sounds, the smells and as you do, remember psalms 118:24. Let us embrace the present ride both on the road and in life and find the joy and peace that comes from being fully present in the moment. What distractions pull you away from the present moment? What practices can you implement to cultivate greater presence in your life?

Prayer: Heavenly Father, thank you for the gift of today. Help me to be present in every moment, to appreciate the beauty of your creation, and to find joy in the journey.

Amen

TAKE A MOMENT EACH DAY TO REFLECT ON THE THINGS YOU'RE THANKFUL FOR

TODAY'S FOCUS

_____
_____

_____

TODAY I AM GRATEFUL FOR...

_____

_____

_____

SOMETHING THAT INSPIRED ME TODAY

PEOPLE I'M GRATEFUL TO HAVE IN MY LIFE

Answered prayers

_____
_____
_____
_____
_____
_____

Notes & Free Thoughts

_____
_____
_____
_____
_____
_____
_____
_____
_____
_____
_____
_____
_____
_____
_____
_____
_____
_____
_____
_____
_____
_____

DAY 5 *scripture*

> For he himself is our peace, who
> has made the two groups one and
> has destroyed the barrier, the
> dividing wall of hostility.
> Ephesians 2:14

Breaking Barriers

In the world of motorcycles, while increasingly welcoming, has historically been a male dominated space. As women riders, we sometimes face subtle (or not-so-subtle) barriers, preconceived notions about our abilities or assumptions about our strength. But Ephesians 2:14 reminds us of a powerful truth to not be discouraged, to be strong and courageous because God will be with us wherever we go.

This verse isn't just about physical strength; it's about inner fortitude. It's about the courage to defy expectations, to challenge stereotypes, and to pursue our passion for riding with confidence. It's about knowing that we are capable not because of our gender, but because of the strength that comes from within, a strength rooted in our faith.

Think about the first time you threw a leg over a motorcycle. Were you nervous? Intimidated? Did you doubt your ability? These feelings are natural but Ephesians 2:14 tells us to push past fear and discouragement. God's command isn't a suggestion, it's a call to action. He is with us empowering us to overcome any obstacle in our path. As women riders we break barriers every time we hit the open road. We challenged the notion that riding is only for men.

We demonstrate our skill, our resilience, our passion for the ride and in doing so we inspire other women to embrace their own dreams to shatter their own glass ceilings and to live their lives to the fullest.

Reflection:. This week remember that you are strong, courageous, and you are not alone. God is with you empowering you to break barriers and to defy expectations, embrace the freedom of the open road. What barriers have you faced? How has your faith helped you overcome these challenges? How can you encourage other women to break barriers in their own lives?

Prayer: Heavenly Father, thank you for the strength and courage you give me.

Help me to be bold and confident in pursuing my passions. Remind me that you are always with me, empowering me to overcome any obstacle.

Amen

DATE

S   M   T   W   T   F   S

TAKE A MOMENT EACH DAY TO REFLECT ON THE THINGS YOU'RE THANKFUL FOR

TODAY'S FOCUS

_____
_____
_____

TODAY I AM GRATEFUL FOR...

_____
_____
_____

SOMETHING THAT INSPIRED ME TODAY

PEOPLE I'M GRATEFUL TO HAVE IN MY LIFE

Answered prayers

_____
_____
_____
_____
_____
_____

Notes & Free Thoughts

_____
_____
_____
_____
_____
_____
_____
_____
_____
_____
_____
_____
_____
_____
_____
_____
_____
_____
_____
_____
_____
_____
_____

DAY 6 *Scripture*

A cheerful heart is good

medicine, but a crushed spirit

dries up the bones.

Proverbs 17:22

Making Memories

Proverbs tells us that a cheerful heart is good, understanding the memories we create, the laughter we share, the bonds we forge-these are the things that nourish our souls and give us the strength to face whatever challenges may come our way. A crushed spirit on the other hand, drains us of energy and leaves us feeling depleted.

The sun on our face, the rumble of the engine beneath us, the winding road stretching ahead-these are the moments that etch themselves into our memories. As women riders, we understand the power of shared experiences, the joy of creating lasting memories with friends, family, and even on solo adventures. Proverbs 17: 22 speaks to the importance of joy, laughter, and a positive outlook, especially when it comes to making memories that will sustain us through life's ups and downs.

As women, we often carry a lot on our shoulders. We juggle responsibilities, manage households, and navigate the complexities of modern life. Riding can be an escape, a chance to let go of this stress and embrace the simple pleasure of the open road. And when we share these experiences with others, the joy is amplified.

Remember, the best rides aren't just about the destination; they're about the journey and the people we share it with. Embrace the open road, embrace the joy, and embrace the opportunity to create memories that will warm your heart for years to come.

Reflection: This week be intentional about creating memories. Invite a friend along for the adventure. Take time to appreciate the beauty of your surroundings. And think about how do you intentionally create positive memories in your life? How does laughter and joy play a role in your overall well-being?

Prayer: Heavenly Father, thank you for the gift of joy. Help me to embrace the opportunity to create lasting memories with loved ones and to cherish the moments of laughter and connection.

Amen

DATE

S M T W T F S

TAKE A MOMENT EACH DAY TO REFLECT ON THE THINGS YOU'RE THANKFUL FOR

TODAY'S FOCUS

_____
_____
_____

TODAY I AM GRATEFUL FOR...

_____
_____
_____

SOMETHING THAT INSPIRED ME TODAY

PEOPLE I'M GRATEFUL TO HAVE IN MY LIFE

Answered prayers

_____
_____
_____
_____
_____
_____

Notes & Free Thoughts

_____

_____

_____

_____

_____

_____

_____

_____

_____

_____

_____

_____

_____

_____

_____

_____

_____

_____

_____

_____

DAY 7 *scripture*

> *I praise you, for I am fearfully and wonderfully made; your works are wonderful, I know that full well.*
> *Psalms 139:14*

Mindfulness on the Move

As the road unfolds, the world rushes by in a blur of colors and sensations. On a motorcycle, we are intimately connected to our surroundings. Acutely aware of every twist and turn, every shift in the wind. Yet, in this fast-paced world, it's easy to become disconnected from ourselves lost in the noise of our thoughts and worries. Psalms 139:14 isn't just about acknowledging God's creation; it's about recognizing the wonder within ourselves. As women, we are complex, multifaceted beings, capable of incredible strength, resilience, and grace. And as women who ride, we embody a unique blend of freedom and focus, navigating the open road with skill and confidence.

Mindfulness, the practice of paying attention to the present moment without judgment, can be a powerful tool for women riders. It allows us to fully engage with the experience of riding, to appreciate the beauty of the landscape, and to connect with our inner selves. It's about being present in the here and now, letting go of distractions, and finding peace in the midst of motion.

Reflection: Mindfulness isn't about emptying our minds; it's about observing our thoughts and feelings without getting carried away by them. It's about acknowledging the beauty of the present moment, the wonder of our own being, and the presence of God in all things.

This week, practice mindfulness on the move. Pay attention to your breath, the feel of the wind on your skin, notice the details of the world around you - the colors, the sounds, the smells. Embrace the present ride both on the road and in life and find the peace and wonder that comes from being fully present in the moment.

Prayer: Heavenly Father, Thank you for creating me fearfully and wonderfully.

Help me to be present in each moment, to appreciate the beauty of your creation, and to find peace in the journey.

Amen.

DATE

S   M   T   W   T   F   S

TAKE A MOMENT EACH DAY TO REFLECT ON THE THINGS YOU'RE THANKFUL FOR

TODAY'S FOCUS

_____

_____

_____

TODAY I AM GRATEFUL FOR...

_____

_____

_____

SOMETHING THAT INSPIRED ME TODAY

PEOPLE I'M GRATEFUL TO HAVE IN MY LIFE

Answered prayers

_____

_____

_____

_____

_____

_____

Notes & Free Thoughts

DAY 8 *Scripture*

> *He makes me lie down in green pastures, he leads me beside quiet waters.*
>
> *Psalm 23:2*

Life can often feel like a storm – a whirlwind of responsibilities, challenges, and uncertainties. Psalm 23:2 offers a comforting image; this verse speaks to the importance of finding stillness, of seeking refuge amidst the storms of life, and of trusting in God's guidance.

As women riders, we understand the need for focus and control. We navigate winding roads, anticipate changing conditions, and make split second decisions that keep us safe. But just as we need to be attentive on the road, we also need to find moments of stillness in our lives, moments where we can reconnect with ourselves, with our faith, and with the peace that comes from surrendering to God's care.

Do you remember the first time you were caught in the rain? I think that's one of the memories you don't ever forget. I was on a poker run. My very first poker run, we were the second stop in and in a downpour of rain. We couldn't see the bike in front of us, but yet we were able to adapt, stay safe, and enjoy the ride.

To this day that was still probably one of the funniest poker runs I have been on. But if we go back and think if it had rained before the ride started would we have even gone out? Probably not.

How many times do we miss something because there's a storm in our way? We forget that God will lead us through. And many times through the storm is when true growth begins and those are the times when God leads us to lie down in green pastures.

Reflection: This week, be mindful of the need for stillness in your life. Take time to pause, to breathe, to connect with your inner self. Find moments of quiet reflection, whether it's during a scenic stop on your ride or in the stillness of your own home. As you do, remember God is with you, even in the midst of the storm. He desires to lead you to green pastures and quiet waters, places where you can find rest, renewal, and the peace that comes from trusting in his loving care. Try to find and create more space for rest and reflection in your daily routine.

Prayer: Heavenly Father, thank you for your promise of rest and renewal.

Help me to find stillness in the midst of the storms of life, to trust in your guidance and to find peace in your presence.

Amen.

DATE

S   M   T   W   T   F   S

TAKE A MOMENT EACH DAY TO REFLECT ON THE THINGS YOU'RE THANKFUL FOR

TODAY'S FOCUS

_____
_____
_____

TODAY I AM GRATEFUL FOR...

_____
_____
_____

SOMETHING THAT INSPIRED ME TODAY

PEOPLE I'M GRATEFUL TO HAVE IN MY LIFE

Answered prayers

_____
_____
_____
_____
_____
_____

Notes & Free Thoughts

_____

_____

_____

_____

_____

_____

_____

_____

_____

_____

_____

_____

_____

_____

_____

_____

_____

DAY 9 *Scripture*

> The path of the righteous is like the morning sun, shining ever brighter till the full light of day.
>
> Proverbs 4:18

Embracing the Learning Curve

Every rider remembers the first time they twisted the throttle, the wobbly start, the tentative lean into the first curve. Learning to ride a motorcycle is a journey, a process of growth and development. There are moments of exhilaration, moments of frustration, and plenty of moments where we feel like we're still finding our footing. Proverbs 4:18 offers a beautiful image for this journey. This verse isn't just about moral righteousness; it's about the path of learning, the journey of growth. As women riders, we understand that mastery takes time, practice, and a willingness to embrace the learning curve. We don't become skilled riders overnight. We learn from our mistakes, we refine our techniques, and we gradually gain confidence with each mile we ride.

These challenges are a normal part of the learning process. Just as the morning sun gradually increases in intensity, our skills and confidence as riders grow overtime. There will be days when you feel like you're making progress, and there will be days when you feel like you're taking 2 steps back. But the key is to keep learning, keep practicing, and keep your eyes on the horizon.

With each ride, with each lesson, with each mile you

conquer, you are moving closer to that "full light of day" - the point where you feel truly comfortable and confident on your bike. It is the same with our faith. We have to learn to be diligent about reading the Bible, finding friends we can confide in, and asking questions. Learning never stops.

Reflection: Remember that every challenge is an opportunity to learn and grow. Don't be afraid to make mistakes, don't be discouraged by setbacks as you reflect this week. Think about some of the biggest challenges you've faced. How have you overcome them? And what did you learn from them?

Prayer: Heavenly Father, Thank you for the journey of learning and growth.

Help me to embrace the learning curve, to be patient with myself, and to trust that my skills and confidence will continue to grow.

Amen.

DATE

S M T W T F S

TAKE A MOMENT EACH DAY TO REFLECT ON THE THINGS YOU'RE THANKFUL FOR

TODAY'S FOCUS

_____
_____
_____

TODAY I AM GRATEFUL FOR...

_____
_____
_____

SOMETHING THAT INSPIRED ME TODAY

PEOPLE I'M GRATEFUL TO HAVE IN MY LIFE

Answered prayers

_____
_____
_____
_____
_____
_____

Notes & Free Thoughts

_____

_____

_____

_____

_____

_____

_____

_____

_____

_____

_____

_____

_____

_____

_____

_____

_____

_____

_____

_____

DAY 10 *scripture*

> *Splendor and majesty are before him; strength and glory are in his sanctuary.*
>
> *Psalms 96:6*

The Beauty of Adventure

As riders, we understand the thrill of exploring new places, of discovering hidden gems, of pushing ourselves beyond our comfort zones. This verse speaks to the awe inspiring beauty of God's creation and the strength we find in his presence, especially when we venture out into the unknown.

The world is full of wonders, from towering mountains to vast deserts, from winding coastal roads to quiet country lanes. As we ride, we become intimately connected to those landscapes, feeling the wind on our faces, smelling the scent of fresh cut grass and witnessing the grandeur of God's handiwork. These experiences fill our souls with a sense of awe and wonder, reminding us of the beauty that surrounds us.

But adventure isn't just about the external landscape; it's also about the internal journey. It's about discovering our own strength, resilience, and courage. It's about pushing past our fears, embracing the unknown, and realizing that we are capable of more than we ever thought possible.

Some 96: 6 tells us that splendor and majesty are before Him. As we explore the world, we encounter that splendor and majesty first hand. We are witnessing the glory of God's creation, and in doing so, we are drawing closer to him.

Reflection: Embrace the beauty of adventure. Explore new routes, challenge yourself to try something new, and allow yourself to be awestruck by the world around you. Really think about what adventure means to you? How has riding allowed you to experience the beauty of the world?

Prayer: Heavenly Father, thank you for the beauty of your creation and for the spirit of adventure within me.

Help me to embrace the open road, to explore the wonders of your world, and to find strength and glory in your presence.

Amen.

DATE

S   M   T   W   T   F   S

TAKE A MOMENT EACH DAY TO REFLECT ON THE THINGS YOU'RE THANKFUL FOR

TODAY'S FOCUS

_____

_____

_____

TODAY I AM GRATEFUL FOR...

_____

_____

_____

SOMETHING THAT INSPIRED ME TODAY

PEOPLE I'M GRATEFUL TO HAVE IN MY LIFE

Answered prayers

_____

_____

_____

_____

_____

Notes & Free Thoughts

_____
_____
_____
_____
_____
_____
_____
_____
_____
_____
_____
_____
_____
_____
_____
_____
_____
_____
_____
_____
_____
_____
_____

♥

DAY 11 *Scripture*

> Therefore, there is now no condemnation for those who are in Christ Jesus.
> Romans 8:1

The Fear of Falling Short

Every rider knows the feeling: the slight wobble, the unexpected gravel, the near miss. The fear of falling short, of making a mistake, of not being good enough, is a common experience, both on and off the motorcycle. As women we may feel this pressure even more acutely, navigating a world that sometimes subtly questions are abilities. But Romans 8: 1 offers a powerful message of hope. This verse speaks to the heart of grace. It reminds us that our worth is not based on our performance, on whether we execute every turn perfectly or avoid every potential hazard. Instead, our value comes from our relationship with Christ. He has already paid the price for our mistakes, for our shortcomings, for our "falls."
We are not defined by our mistakes. Our identity is rooted in Christ's love and forgiveness. This doesn't mean we shouldn't strive to improve our skills or take safety seriously; but it does mean that we can let go of the fear of falling short. Knowing wholeheartedly that we are loved and accepted, regardless of our performance. We often face internal and external pressures to be perfect. We may compare ourselves to others, worry about what others think, or struggle with self-doubt. But Romans 8: 1 offers a powerful antidote to these fears.

It reminds us that we are free from condemnation, free to learn, free to grow, and free to enjoy the ride without the weight of perfectionism.
Ride with confidence, knowing that you are not defined by your shortcomings, but by the love of Christ.

Reflection: Remember that you are loved, you are forgiven, and you are free. Embrace the learning process, accept that mistakes will happen, and trust in the grace that covers all things. How does the fear of falling short affect you? How do you respond to yourself when you make a mistake? And how can you embrace the message of Romans 8:1 in your life?

Prayer: Heavenly Father, thank you for your grace and forgiveness. Help me to let go of the fear of falling short, to embrace the learning process, and to ride with confidence, knowing that I am loved and accepted.

Amen.

DATE

S M T W T F S

TAKE A MOMENT EACH DAY TO REFLECT ON THE THINGS YOU'RE THANKFUL FOR

TODAY'S FOCUS

_____
_____
_____

TODAY I AM GRATEFUL FOR...

_____
_____
_____

SOMETHING THAT INSPIRED ME TODAY	PEOPLE I'M GRATEFUL TO HAVE IN MY LIFE

Answered prayers

_____
_____
_____
_____
_____
_____

Notes & Free Thoughts

_____

_____

_____

_____

_____

_____

_____

_____

_____

_____

_____

_____

_____

_____

_____

_____

_____

♥

DAY 12 *Scripture*

> But he said to me, "My grace is sufficient for you, for my power is made perfect in weakness." Therefore, I will boast all of them were gladly about my weaknesses, so that Christ's power may rest on me.
>
> Corinthians 12:9

Power & Grace

Riding requires skill, focus, and a certain amount of strength, both physical and mental. We may sometimes feel pressure to prove ourselves, to demonstrate that we are just as capable as anyone else. But 2 Corinthians 12:9 offers a powerful reminder: "My grace is sufficient for you, for my power is made perfect in weakness." This verse speaks to the heart of true strength. It reminds us that our power doesn't come from our own abilities alone, but from the grace of God working within us. It's in our moments of weakness, when we acknowledge our limitations, that God's power can truly shine through.

We often embody a beautiful combination of power and grace. We are strong and capable, yet we also possess a certain elegance and fluidity; this balance reflects the truth of 2 Corinthians 12:9. Our strength is not about brute force; it's about tapping into the grace that empowers us, the grace that makes us capable of far more than we could ever achieve on our own. This verse also speaks to the importance of humility. It encourages us to boast in our weaknesses, not because we revel in our shortcomings, but because it's in those moments that we recognize our dependence on God.

It's when we let go of our pride and acknowledge our need for help that we open ourselves up to the power of God's grace.

Reflection: Think about a time when you faced a challenge on your bike. Maybe it was a difficult road condition, a mechanical issue, or a moment of self-doubt. How did you respond? Did you try to muscle through it, relying on your own strength? Or did you acknowledge your vulnerability and ask for help? This week, think about how you have experienced the power of grace? How can you cultivate greater humility in your life?

Prayer: Heavenly Father, thank you for your grace, which is sufficient for me.

Help me to embrace my weaknesses, to rely on your power, and to ride with confidence, knowing that you are with me every step of the way.

Amen.

DATE

S M T W T F S

TAKE A MOMENT EACH DAY TO REFLECT ON THE THINGS YOU'RE THANKFUL FOR

TODAY'S FOCUS

_____
_____
_____

TODAY I AM GRATEFUL FOR...

_____
_____
_____

SOMETHING THAT INSPIRED ME TODAY

PEOPLE I'M GRATEFUL TO HAVE IN MY LIFE

Answered prayers

_____
_____
_____
_____
_____
_____

Notes & Free Thoughts

DAY 13 *Scripture*

> Consider pure joy, my brothers and sisters, whenever you face trials of various kinds, because you know that the testing of your faith produces endurance. Let endurance complete its work so that you may be mature and complete, not lacking anything.
>
> Matthew 7:13 -14

Embracing the Unexpected

"Joy" might seem like an odd response to a flat tire in the middle of nowhere, but James isn't suggesting we celebrate hardship itself. Instead, he's encouraging us to shift our perspective. He reminds us that even the unexpected, even the difficult, can be opportunities for growth, for building resilience, and for deepening our faith.

We embody a spirit of adventure and in the we will face trials, both on and off the bike, test our faith and produce endurance. They teach us to rely on our inner strength, to tap into our resourcefulness, and to trust that even in the midst of the unexpected, God is with us. He is using these experiences to shape us, to mold us, and to make us more like him.

Reflection: This week, embrace the unexpected, knowing that it is an opportunity for growth, for building endurance, and for becoming the woman you were created to be. Think about how having unexpected challenges in your life helped you grow? How can you cultivate a spirit of joy in the face of the unexpected? And how does your faith help you navigate the unexpected twists and turns of life?

Prayer: Heavenly Father, thank you for your presence in the midst of the unexpected.

Help me to embrace the challenges that come my way, to learn from them, and to grow stronger and more complete through them.

Amen.

DATE

S   M   T   W   T   F   S

TAKE A MOMENT EACH DAY TO REFLECT ON THE THINGS YOU'RE THANKFUL FOR

TODAY'S FOCUS

_____
_____
_____

TODAY I AM GRATEFUL FOR...

_____
_____
_____

SOMETHING THAT INSPIRED ME TODAY

PEOPLE I'M GRATEFUL TO HAVE IN MY LIFE

Answered prayers

_____
_____
_____
_____
_____
_____

Notes & Free Thoughts

_____

_____

_____

_____

_____

_____

_____

_____

_____

_____

_____

_____

_____

_____

_____

_____

_____

_____

DAY 14 *scripture*

> That everyone may eat and drink
> and find satisfaction in all their
> toil – this is the gift of God.
> Ecclesiastes 3:13

Investing in your passion

Riding is more than just a hobby; it's a passion, it's part of who we are. Ecclesiastes 3:13 offers a simple yet profound truth: this verse speaks to the importance of finding joy and fulfillment in the things we do, including the passion that ignites our souls.

As women who ride, we know the dedication it takes to pursue this passion. We invest time, money, and energy into our bikes, our gear, and our skills. We brave the elements, overcome challenges, and consistently strive to improve our riding abilities. But it's not just about the effort; it's about the deep sense of fulfillment that comes from doing something we love.

Sometimes we may question whether we're "justified" in spending time and resources on our hobbies. We may feel guilty about taking time for ourselves, especially when we have so many other responsibilities. But Ecclesiastes reminds us that finding satisfaction in our toil, in the things we invest our time and energy into, is a gift. It's a part of God's plan for our lives.

Embrace your passion for riding. Invest in it, nurture it, and allow it to bring you joy and fulfillment. Know that the satisfaction you find in riding is a gift, a blessing, in a part of what makes you uniquely you.

Reflection: Think about what riding brings to your life. Does it give you a sense of freedom? Does it connect you with nature? Does it challenge you to grow and learn? Does it provide a community of like-minded women? These are the gifts that come from investing in our passions. It's not just about the activity itself; it's about the impact it has on our lives. This week really think about how you can silence the inner critic that questions the value of pursuing your passions. What can you remind yourself of when the guilt starts to surface?

Prayer: Heavenly Father, thank you for the gift of passion and for the joy it brings.

Help me to embrace the challenge and to grow and learn. Please help me to silence the inner critic that makes me question my passion. Help me to invest in my passion wholeheartedly, and to find satisfaction in all my toil.

Amen.

S   M   T   W   T   F   S

TAKE A MOMENT EACH DAY TO REFLECT ON THE THINGS YOU'RE THANKFUL FOR

TODAY'S FOCUS

_____
_____
_____
_____

TODAY I AM GRATEFUL FOR...

_____
_____
_____
_____

SOMETHING THAT INSPIRED ME TODAY

PEOPLE I'M GRATEFUL TO HAVE IN MY LIFE

Answered prayers

_____
_____
_____
_____
_____
_____

Notes & Free Thoughts

_____

_____

_____

_____

_____

_____

_____

_____

_____

_____

_____

_____

_____

_____

_____

_____

_____

_____

DAY 15 *scripture*

The rich rule over the poor, and the borrower is servant to the lender.

Proverbs 22:7

Avoiding Debt

The dream of owning a motorcycle, the right gear, and the ability to travel can sometimes lead to financial temptation. Proverbs 22:7 offers a sobering reminder: "the rich rule over the poor, and the borrower is servant to the lender." This verse speaks to the importance of financial wisdom, especially when it comes to pursuing our passions.

We understand the investment required to enjoy this activity. From the cost of the bike itself to insurance, maintenance, riding gear, and travel expenses. It's easy to get caught up in the excitement and desire to have it all, leading to overspending and accumulating debt. Proverbs 22:7 isn't about shaming those who have debt. It's about recognizing the power dynamics at play. When we owe money, our choices become limited, and our financial freedom is compromised. This doesn't mean we can't ever borrow money, but it does mean we should be mindful of the potential consequences and avoid unnecessary debt.

We value our independence and freedom, that is why we ride. Financial freedom is an essential part of that. By being responsible with our finances, we maintain control over our lives and our ability to pursue our passions.

We avoid becoming "servants to the lender" and instead remain masters of our own destiny.

Reflection: Think about your own financial habits. Have you ever financed a motorcycle purchase without carefully considering the long-term costs? Have you ever put riding gear or accessories on a credit card without a clear plan for repayment? Have you ever skipped necessary maintenance to save money in the short term, potentially leading to bigger expenses down the road? This week, think about your financial goals. Be mindful of your spending habits. Make a plan to avoid or reduce your debt.

Prayer: Heavenly Father, help me to be a wise steward of my finances, to avoid unnecessary debt, and to avoid being a servant to the lender. Help me to be wise with my spending and prioritize needs over wants.

Amen.

TAKE A MOMENT EACH DAY TO REFLECT ON THE THINGS YOU'RE THANKFUL FOR

TODAY'S FOCUS

_____
_____
_____

TODAY I AM GRATEFUL FOR...

_____
_____
_____

SOMETHING THAT INSPIRED ME TODAY

PEOPLE I'M GRATEFUL TO HAVE IN MY LIFE

Answered prayers

_____
_____
_____
_____
_____
_____

Notes & Free Thoughts

_____
_____
_____
_____
_____
_____
_____
_____
_____
_____
_____
_____
_____
_____
_____
_____
_____
_____
_____

DAY 16 *Scripture*

> Cast all your anxiety on him
> because he cares for you.
> 1 Peter 5:7

Saddlebags and spiritual baggage:
Letting go of burdens

Every rider knows the importance of packing light. Saddlebags are only so big, and too much weight can throw off your balance, slow you down, and make the ride harder than it needs to be. You learn quickly what you really need and what can be left behind.

Spiritually, we carry saddle bags too-only they're not filled with clothes and gear. They're packed with guilt, fear, regret, worry, unforgiveness, shame, which makes it difficult to ride freely in the joy and purpose God has for us.

But there's good news: God never meant for you to carry all of that. He invites you to offload every burden, every piece of spiritual baggage, and leave it with him. He's strong enough to carry it. He wants you to be free-to lean into the turns, and ride with peace, to move forward without all that weight.

Letting go might mean forgiving someone, even if they don't deserve it. It might mean trusting God with something you've been trying to control. It might mean finally believing that his grace really is enough-even for you.

Reflection: Take a moment to look into your spiritual saddlebags.

What's been riding with you for too long?
What burden is God asking you to release?

Prayer: Heavenly Father, you know what I've been carrying. Some of it I've dragged with me for years. Today, I lay it all at your feet - my fears, my failures, my pain.

Thank you that I don't have to carry it anymore. Teach me to trust you with every burden. Let me ride free, light, and full of your peace.

Amen

DATE

S   M   T   W   T   F   S

TAKE A MOMENT EACH DAY TO REFLECT ON THE THINGS YOU'RE THANKFUL FOR

TODAY'S FOCUS

_____
_____
_____

_____

TODAY I AM GRATEFUL FOR...

_____
_____
_____

SOMETHING THAT INSPIRED ME TODAY

PEOPLE I'M GRATEFUL TO HAVE IN MY LIFE

Answered prayers

_____
_____
_____
_____
_____
_____

Notes & Free Thoughts

_____
_____
_____
_____
_____
_____
_____
_____
_____
_____
_____
_____
_____
_____
_____
_____
_____
_____

♥

DAY 17 *Scripture*

> *You will also decree a thing, and it will be established for you; and light will shine on your ways.*
>
> *Job 22:28*

Faith Beyond the Horizon

There's something about riding a long stretch of road
with nothing but the horizon in front of you. You don't
always know what's around the next bend or over the
next hill-but you trust your bike, your experience, and the
road beneath you. Riding, like faith, is often about
moving forward even when you can't see what's ahead.
Job 22: 28 reminds us that what we speak in faith-what
we declare in alignment with God's will-can shape our
reality. It's not about demanding our way, but about
declaring God's truth over our lives with boldness and
belief. That kind of faith moves mountains, even the ones
we haven't seen yet.
Faith beyond the horizon is trusting that even if your path
looks dim now, light will shine when it's time. It's riding
into uncertainty with a heart full of belief that God is
already ahead of you, clearing the way. When the future
feels foggy, when life throws unexpected turns, or when
you're tempted to pull over and just stop - remember that
faith doesn't require a clear view, just a clear trust in the
One who's leading you.

Reflection: What area of your life feels uncertain or
hidden beyond the horizon right now? How can you use
your faith to declare mountains be moved with your faith?

Prayer: Heavenly Father, thank you that even when I can't see what's ahead, you do.

Help me to declare your promises with boldness and to ride in faith, not fear. Shine your light on my path and lead me forward, one mile at a time.

I trust you with every turn, every hill, and every unknown.

Amen.

S   M   T   W   T   F   S

TAKE A MOMENT EACH DAY TO REFLECT ON THE THINGS YOU'RE THANKFUL FOR

TODAY'S FOCUS

_____

_____

_____

TODAY I AM GRATEFUL FOR...

_____

_____

_____

SOMETHING THAT INSPIRED ME TODAY | PEOPLE I'M GRATEFUL TO HAVE IN MY LIFE

Answered prayers

_____

_____

_____

_____

_____

_____

Notes & Free Thoughts

_____
_____
_____
_____
_____
_____
_____
_____
_____
_____
_____
_____
_____
_____
_____
_____
_____
_____
_____
_____
_____

DAY 1 *Scripture*

Enter through the narrow gate

for wide is the gate and broad is

a road that leads to destruction,

and many enter through it but

small is the gate and narrow is

the road that leads to life and

only a few find it.

Matthew 7:13-14

The Open Road and The Narrow Gate

To anyone who has had the joy of riding a motorcycle, you know the allure of the open road, and how it beckons us with its promise of adventure. It's a place where worries fade, where the present moment is all that matters. We feel a sense of power and control navigating the curves and conquering challenges and this freedom can be intoxicating. We can easily get caught up in the thrill of the ride in the pursuit of speed and excitement and neglect the spiritual side of the journey.

With its freedom also comes the feel of wind in our hair, the miles stretching before us, the smells of fresh cut grass or honeysuckles. It gives us the freedom to see for miles with no obstruction, but we know around every curve or over a big hill there are dangers on the road and so are there dangers in life. The Bible speaks of a narrow gate, a path to righteousness that can be challenging to follow. It can be hard being a woman and even harder being a woman who rides. As riders, we crave that sense of liberation, the feeling of escaping the constraints of everyday life but true freedom, the kind that truly satisfies, isn't just about the open road. It's about finding freedom in Christ.

Reflection: On your next ride remember to seek both the freedom of the open road and the freedom found in Christ. May your journey be filled with joy, adventure, and a deep sense of peace.

Prayer:
Heavenly Father, as I prepare to embark on this journey I place my trust in your loving hands.

Guide my hands and feet, keep my mind alert and focused, and protect me from harm. May the wind in my hair be a reminder of your constant presence, and the open road a symbol of the endless possibilities that await.

Grant me courage and wisdom on this ride, and may my spirit be uplifted by your grace.

Amen.

S   M   T   W   T   F   S

TAKE A MOMENT EACH DAY TO REFLECT ON THE THINGS YOU'RE THANKFUL FOR

TODAY'S FOCUS

_____
_____
_____

TODAY I AM GRATEFUL FOR...

_____
_____
_____

SOMETHING THAT INSPIRED ME TODAY.

PEOPLE I'M GRATEFUL TO HAVE IN MY LIFE

Answered prayers

_____
_____
_____
_____
_____
_____

Notes & Free Thoughts

_____

_____

_____

_____

_____

_____

_____

_____

_____

_____

_____

_____

_____

_____

_____

_____

_____

_____

_____

_____

♥

DAY 19 *scripture*

She is clothed with strength and dignity; she can laugh at the days to come.

Job 22:28

The Beauty of Confidence

The beauty in a woman who can throw her leg over a bike, straightens her helmet, and rides with purpose. It's not just the machine beneath her-it's the strength within her. Confidence isn't about being fearless or having it all figured out. It's about knowing who you are, and even more importantly, whose you are.

As Proverbs 31: 25 paints a picture of a woman who isn't shaken by the unknown. She is clothed-not in leather or denim-but in strength and dignity. She laughs at the future, not because life is easy, but because she knows that whatever comes, she's not riding alone. Confidence rooted in Christ is different from what the world offers. It's not about image, approval, or even performance. It's about identity. When you know that God goes before you, walks beside you, and has your back-you ride it differently.

There's a unique beauty in that kind of confidence. It draws others in. It says" if God can do this in me, he can do it in you too."

Reflection: Throw your shoulders back. Start the engine. Ride bold. Because the same God who created the stars, crafted you-with purpose, with strength,

and with a confidence that shines through you. How can you encourage another woman to ride in God-given confidence today?

Prayer: Heavenly Father, Thank you for clothing me with strength and dignity.

Remind me that I don't have to fear the future, because you are already there. Teach me to write in confidence-not in myself, but in who I am in you.

Help me be a light and an encouragement to others who need to see the beauty of bold faith.

Amen.

S   M   T   W   T   F   S

TAKE A MOMENT EACH DAY TO REFLECT ON THE THINGS YOU'RE THANKFUL FOR

TODAY'S FOCUS

_____
_____
_____

TODAY I AM GRATEFUL FOR...

_____
_____
_____

SOMETHING THAT INSPIRED ME TODAY

PEOPLE I'M GRATEFUL TO HAVE IN MY LIFE

Answered prayers.

_____
_____
_____
_____
_____
_____

Notes & Free Thoughts

DAY 20 *scripture*

One who has unreliable friends soon comes to ruin, but there is a friend who sticks closer than a brother.

Proverbs 18:24

The Beauty of Sisterhood

There's something sacred about sisterhood- especially among women who ride. It's more than shared miles and matching leather; it's the bond that forms when hearts ride side by side through the twists and turns of life. Real sisterhood isn't just about riding together-it's about doing life together.

Proverbs 18: 24 reminds us that not all friendships are created equal. Some are surface level. They are there when times are good but gone when the ride gets rough. But there is a deeper kind of friendship that reflects the heart of God. The kind of sister who sticks closer than a brother, the one who checks in, prays with you, shows up when it matters, and isn't afraid to speak truth in love. God created us for connection. We're not meant to ride solo through life. Sisterhood is his gift-a place where we find encouragement, accountability, laughter, and healing. It's in sisterhood that we grow stronger, bolder, and more rooted in Christ.

So treasure your sisters on the road and off. Be that ride or die kind of friend who lifts others up, listens without judgment, and loves fiercely. Together we ride stronger.

Reflection: Who are the sisters in your life who stick closer than a brother?

How can you invest more deeply in those relationships?

Prayer: Heavenly Father, thank you for the gift of true sisterhood.

Help me to be the kind of friend who loves well, encourages deeply, and sticks close no matter what.

Teach me to cherish the woman you've placed in my life and to ride this journey with love, loyalty, and grace.

Amen.

DATE

S M T W T F S

TAKE A MOMENT EACH DAY TO REFLECT ON THE THINGS YOU'RE THANKFUL FOR

TODAY'S FOCUS

_____
_____
_____

_____

TODAY I AM GRATEFUL FOR...

_____
_____
_____

_____

SOMETHING THAT INSPIRED ME TODAY

PEOPLE I'M GRATEFUL TO HAVE IN MY LIFE

Answered prayers

_____
_____
_____
_____
_____
_____

Notes & Free Thoughts

_____

_____

_____

_____

_____

_____

_____

_____

_____

_____

_____

_____

_____

_____

_____

_____

♥

DAY 21 *Scripture*

Whether you turn to the right or to the left, your ears will hear a voice behind you, saying,' this is the way; walking it.

Isaiah 30:21

Trusting your Intuition

Out on the open road, Sometimes you just know when to ease up on the throttle, when to pull over, or when to take a turn that wasn't part of the original plan. That deep sense-call it gut feeling, inner voice, or intuition-often whispers what logic can't explain. As women, especially women of faith, we know that intuition is more than just a feeling. When we're walking closely with God, it becomes a way he speaks to our hearts.

Isaiah 30:21 paints a powerful picture of divine guidance: a voice behind you, gently directing your steps. That's the Holy Spirit-God's presence not just beside you, but within you, nudging you in the right direction. Trusting your intuition when it's grounded in God's word and prayer, is really about trusting his voice speaking through your spirit.

The more time you spend with God-on and off the bike-the more clearly you begin to recognize that voice. And the more you trust it, the more confident you become in every turn you take. So the next time your heart pulls in a certain direction, pause and listen. That holy knowledge might just be God saying,: "This is the way-ride into it."

Reflection: Think about a time you have had a moment where your intuition led you in a way that clearly aligned with God's plan.

How can you make space in your life to hear God's quiet direction more clearly?

Prayer: Heavenly Father, thank you for guiding me even when the road ahead isn't clear.

Help me to recognize your voice above all the noise. Teach me to trust those quiet nudges that come from walking with you.

Let my intuition be shaped by your spirit and confirmed by your peace. I want to ride with confidence knowing you are directing every mile.

Amen.

TAKE A MOMENT EACH DAY TO REFLECT ON THE THINGS YOU'RE THANKFUL FOR

TODAY'S FOCUS

TODAY I AM GRATEFUL FOR...

SOMETHING THAT INSPIRED ME TODAY

PEOPLE I'M GRATEFUL TO HAVE IN MY LIFE

Answered prayers

Notes & Free Thoughts

_____

_____

_____

_____

_____

_____

_____

_____

_____

_____

_____

_____

_____

_____

_____

_____

_____

_____

DAY 22 *Scripture*

> *Jesus answered, it is written: Man shall not live on bread alone, but on every word that comes from the mouth of God.*
>
> *Matthew 4:4*

Fueling the Journey

Every rider knows you can't go far on an empty tank. No matter how beautiful your bike is or how clear the skies are, without fuel, you're going nowhere. The same is true for your soul.

In Matthew 4: 4, Jesus reminds us that we aren't just physical beings, we're spiritual ones too. And just like your bike needs fuel for the ride, your spirit needs the word of God to keep moving forward. Life throws curves, delays, and detours and if you're running on fumes spiritually drained and emotionally depleted it's easy to stall out.

God's word isn't just a nice pick me up. It's essential nourishment for the soul. It strengthens you when you are weak, speaks truth when lies creep in, and lights the way when the road gets dark. It's the fuel that keeps your faith engine running strong.

So today, before you move up and hit the road, fill up. Spending time in scripture. Let God's promises saturate your spirit like premium fuel. Because a well fueled rider doesn't just endure the journey-she enjoys it!

Reflection: Think about what kind of fuel have you been running on lately? How does time in God's word change your mindset and energy for the day?

Prayer: Heavenly Father, Thank you for your word, it's the fuel my spirit needs every day.

Help me to not rely on my own strength, but to fill up on your truth regularly.

Remind me that your word gives me power, peace, and purpose for every mile of this journey.

Amen.

TAKE A MOMENT EACH DAY TO REFLECT ON THE THINGS YOU'RE THANKFUL FOR

TODAY'S FOCUS

_____
_____
_____

TODAY I AM GRATEFUL FOR...

_____
_____
_____

SOMETHING THAT INSPIRED ME TODAY

PEOPLE I'M GRATEFUL TO HAVE IN MY LIFE

Answered prayers

_____
_____
_____
_____
_____
_____

Notes & Free Thoughts

♥

DAY 23 *scripture*

> *Trust in the Lord with all your heart and lean not on your own understanding; in all your ways submit to him, and he will make your paths straight.*
>
> *Proverbs 3:5-6*

Finding Balance

Balance is everything when you're riding. Lean too far one way, we overcorrect the other, and you risk a fall. The same is true in life. We often try to balance it all, family, work, friendships, faith-relying on our own understanding to keep everything upright. But real balance comes from surrender, not control.

Proverbs reminds us that balance starts with trust. When we stop trying to figure everything out on our own and lean into gods of wisdom instead, he brings clarity to our path. Trusting him doesn't mean life will be free of bumps or turns, it means you'll be steadied by his presence through them.

When you ride, you learn to let go of tension and trust the bike to move with you. It's a rhythm of give and take, of leaning in and letting go. That's what walking or riding with God is like. When he is at the center everything else aligns.

So today, check your posture on the bike and in your spirit. Are you leaning on your own understanding, or are you trusting the one who knows every turn ahead? True balance begins when you let him lead.

Reflection: In what areas of life are you struggling to find balance right now?

Are you trying to control things that God is asking you to trust him with? And what would it look like to release control and lean into God's understanding?

Prayer: Heavenly Father, I confess that I often try to keep everything in balance by my own strength.

Help me to trust you fully, to let go of control, and to submit every part of my journey to you.

Teach me the beauty of balance that comes from walking-and riding-with you.

Amen.

S   M   T   W   T   F   S

TAKE A MOMENT EACH DAY TO REFLECT ON THE THINGS YOU'RE THANKFUL FOR

TODAY'S FOCUS

_____
_____
_____

TODAY I AM GRATEFUL FOR...

_____
_____
_____

SOMETHING THAT INSPIRED ME TODAY

PEOPLE I'M GRATEFUL TO HAVE IN MY LIFE

Answered prayers

_____
_____
_____
_____
_____
_____

Notes & Free Thoughts

_____
_____
_____
_____
_____
_____
_____
_____
_____
_____
_____
_____
_____
_____
_____
_____
_____
_____

♥

DAY 24 *scripture*

> *We demolish arguments and every pretension that sets itself up against the knowledge of God, and we take captive every thought to make it obedient to Christ.*
>
> *2 Corinthians 10:5*

There's a unique kind of freedom that comes with riding. The wind in your face and nothing but the road ahead. But even the most confident rider can struggle with insecurity when the helmet comes off. Doubt creeps in quietly: Am I enough? Do I belong? What if I fail? Insecurity isn't just about how we feel, it's about what we believe. And more often than not, those feelings come from thoughts that don't line up with God's truth. That's why 2nd Corinthians 10:5 it's such a powerful weapon. It reminds us that we don't have to accept every thought that enters our mind. We can take it captive, measure it against what God says and make it obey Christ.

God says you are fearfully and wonderfully made. He says you're chosen, loved, equipped and called. When your thoughts say otherwise, it's time to fight back not with fists but by faith.

So the next time insecurity shows up on the road, at work, in a relationship, pause and ask, "Is this thought from God, or is it a lie I need to let go of?" Replace the lies with truth. Ride in the confidence of who you are in Christ, not in what the world says about you.

Reflection: What insecurities have you been silently carrying? What truth from God's word can replace the lies you believed?

Practice by taking one thought captive today and speaking God's truth over it.

Prayer: Heavenly Father, You see every part of me even the hidden insecurities and you love me completely.

Help me to recognize the lies I've believed and replace them with your truth.

Teach me to take every thought captive and make it obedient to you. I want to ride through life with confidence, knowing my identity is found in you.

Amen.

DATE

S M T W T F S

TAKE A MOMENT EACH DAY TO REFLECT ON THE THINGS YOU'RE THANKFUL FOR

TODAY'S FOCUS

_____
_____
_____

TODAY I AM GRATEFUL FOR...

_____
_____
_____

SOMETHING THAT INSPIRED ME TODAY

PEOPLE I'M GRATEFUL TO HAVE IN MY LIFE

Answered prayers

_____
_____
_____
_____
_____
_____

Notes & Free Thoughts

DAY 25 *scripture*

> *I can do all things through Christ who strengthens me.*
>
> *Philippians 4:13*

Strength in the Saddle

There's a special kind of strength required to ride a strength that's physical, mental, and emotional. Whether you're handling a heavy bike, navigating tough terrain, or facing a long ride ahead, you need balance, endurance, and courage. But the deepest strength doesn't come from the body or even the will it comes from Christ.

Philippians 4: 13 isn't just a motivational slogan; it's a declaration of dependence. Paul wrote these words from a place of hardship, not ease. He had learned that true strength shows up when we admit our weakness and lean fully on Jesus.

You may feel strong some days and shaky on others. Life throws unexpected curves, loss, fear, disappointment, exhaustion. But no matter what the road looks like, you don't ride alone. Christ is your strength in every situation. He gives you what you need, mile by mile.

So when you swing your leg over the saddle, remember it's not just your strength that carries you forward... it's His. And with Him, there is no road you can't face, no challenge too steep, for through Christ all things are possible.

Reflection: Where in your life do you need Christ's strength the most right now? How has he shown up for you in hard or uncertain times? What would change if you fully relied on his strength instead of your own?

Prayer: Heavenly Father, thank you for being my strength in every situation.

When I feel weak or unsteady, remind me that I can do all things through you.

Help me to ride, and live with courage, knowing that your power is made perfect in my weakness.

Amen.

DATE

S M T W T F S

TAKE A MOMENT EACH DAY TO REFLECT ON THE THINGS YOU'RE THANKFUL FOR

TODAY'S FOCUS

_____
_____
_____

TODAY I AM GRATEFUL FOR...

_____
_____
_____

SOMETHING THAT INSPIRED ME TODAY	PEOPLE I'M GRATEFUL TO HAVE IN MY LIFE

Answered prayers

_____
_____
_____
_____
_____
_____

Notes & Free Thoughts

DAY 26 *scripture*

> *...for it is by grace you have been saved, through faith–and this is not from yourselves, it is the gift of God–not by works, so that no one can boast.*
>
> *Ephesians 2:8-9*

Gift of Grace

In a world that teaches us to prove ourselves, grace whispers," you don't have to." It lifts the burden of trying to be good enough and replaces it with the peace of knowing you already are because of Jesus.

Ephesians 2: 8-9 reminds us that salvation isn't something we can earn with perfect performance, polished prayers, where there is a spotless past. It's a gift. Freely given. Unearned. Undeserved. And it changes everything.

Every writer knows the feeling of receiving something you didn't earn-like a stranger who stops to help you fix a flat, or a friend who picks up the tab at the next gas stop. You didn't ask, and you certainly didn't deserve it but it showed up anyway. That's grace.

On the ride of life, you'll hit rough patches. You'll mess up. You'll stall out. But grace is the steady hand that helps you back up. It's the reason you can ride forward without shame and with full confidence in God's love.

So today, receive the gift. Don't try to earn what's already been freely given. Let grace be the fuel for your journey not guilt, not striving, not fear. Just grace.

Reflection: Do you ever feel like you have to" earn" God's love or approval?

How does it feel to know that grace is a gift, not a reward? How can you extend grace to yourself and others today?

Prayer: Heavenly Father, thank you for the gift of grace. Remind me that I don't have to earn your love, it's already mine.

Help me to ride in that freedom, with a heart full of gratitude and peace.

Let grace shape how I see myself, how I live, and how I love.

Amen.

S   M   T   W   T   F   S

TAKE A MOMENT EACH DAY TO REFLECT ON THE THINGS YOU'RE THANKFUL FOR

TODAY'S FOCUS

_____
_____
_____

TODAY I AM GRATEFUL FOR...

_____
_____
_____

SOMETHING THAT INSPIRED ME TODAY

PEOPLE I'M GRATEFUL TO HAVE IN MY LIFE

Answered prayers

_____
_____
_____
_____
_____
_____

Notes & Free Thoughts

❤

DAY 27 *scripture*

Speak up for those who cannot speak for themselves, for the rights of all who are destitute. Speak up and judge fairly; defend the rights of the poor and needy.

Proverbs 31:8-9

Finding your Voice

There's power in a woman who knows how to use her voice. Whether it's the roar of an engine for the quiet strength in a conversation, your voice matters. Proverbs 31:8-9 reminds us that finding your voice isn't just about speaking up for yourself, it's about speaking up for others, for truth, for justice, and for what's right.

As women who ride, we know the importance of being bold. It takes courage to hit the open road, And it takes just as much courage to stand up, speak out, and live with conviction. But too often, insecurity or fear of judgment keeps us silent. God didn't create you to stay quiet, he gave you a voice for a reason.

Your voice can encourage, empower, protect, and inspire. It can lift up someone who's struggling and challenge injustice where it stands. When you speak, let your words reflect the heart of God strong, compassionate, and true.

So today, whether you're riding solo or rolling with your sisters, remember: your voice carries weight. Don't be afraid to use it. Someone might be waiting for your words to remind them of their worth, their strength, or their hope.

Reflection: Where in your life do you feel called to speak up but haven't yet? How can you use your voice to stand up for someone else this week? What fears hold you back from speaking, and what truth from God can help silence those fears?

Prayer: Heavenly Father, Thank you for giving me a voice and a purpose.

Help me to use my words wisely and boldly. Show me where I need to speak up not just for myself, but for those who can't.

Let my voice echo your truth and love in every conversation in every cause.

Amen.

S   M   T   W   T   F   S

TAKE A MOMENT EACH DAY TO REFLECT ON THE THINGS YOU'RE THANKFUL FOR

TODAY'S FOCUS

_____
_____
_____

TODAY I AM GRATEFUL FOR...

_____
_____
_____

SOMETHING THAT INSPIRED ME TODAY

PEOPLE I'M GRATEFUL TO HAVE IN MY LIFE

Answered prayers

_____
_____
_____
_____
_____
_____

Notes & Free Thoughts

_____

_____

_____

_____

_____

_____

_____

_____

_____

_____

_____

_____

_____

_____

_____

_____

_____

_____

_____

_____

DAY 28 *Scripture*

> For God so loved the world that
> he gave his one and only son, that
> whoever believes in him shall not
> perish but have eternal life.
>
> John 3:16

Resting in Gods Love

There's something sacred about the open road. The hum of the engine, the wind against your skin, and the miles stretching out before you; it's a freedom things can match. But even in the thrill of the ride, our souls sometimes carry heavy loads. The pressure to be strong, to keep pushing, to prove ourselves especially in a world that doesn't always understand a woman who rides her own path.

But here's the truth: you don't have to ride alone.

John 3: 16 reminds us of the depth of God's love. Not a passive love, but an active, sacrificial one. He loved you so much that he gave His son for you. Not because you earned it. Not because you have it all together. But simply because you are His.

Today, take a moment to rest not just your body, but your soul. Pull over from the business of life, take off the helmet of performance and pressure, and let yourself be still in his presence. You are fully known and fully loved by the one who created the mountains you ride through and the stars you ride under.

His love is your safe haven, your rest stop in the wild ride of life.

FAITH ON TWO WHEELS

Reflection: What areas of your life feel the most restless right now?

How can you intentionally invite God's love into those spaces and allow yourself to truly rest in Him?

Prayer: Heavenly Father, thank you for loving me with a love that doesn't change, even when I do.

Help me to find rest in your presence today.

Teach me to slow down and simply receive your love. I don't have to earn it; I just have to accept it.

Let me ride with the confidence that I am deeply loved by you.

Amen.

DATE

S M T W T F S

TAKE A MOMENT EACH DAY TO REFLECT ON THE THINGS
YOU'RE THANKFUL FOR

TODAY'S FOCUS

_____
_____
_____

TODAY I AM GRATEFUL FOR...

_____
_____
_____

SOMETHING THAT INSPIRED ME TODAY

PEOPLE I'M GRATEFUL TO HAVE
IN MY LIFE

Answered prayers

_____
_____
_____
_____
_____
_____

Notes & Free Thoughts

_____
_____
_____
_____
_____
_____
_____
_____
_____
_____
_____
_____
_____
_____
_____
_____

DAY 29 *Scripture*

> *So may all your enemies perish, Lord! But may all who love you be like the sun when it rises in its strength." Then the land had peace for 40 years.*
>
> *Judges 5:31*

Leading with Courage & Wisdom

Deborah was no ordinary woman. She was a prophet, a judge, and a warrior called by God to lead at a time when others hesitated. When fear and uncertainty held back many, Deborah stepped forward, not with pride, but with courage rooted in God's wisdom.

As women who ride, we often carry that same spirit. We blaze our own trail, stand tall in the face of challenges, and push through the noise to follow the call placed on our lives. But like Deborah, we aren't strong on our own. Our courage and wisdom come from the one who rides beside us-Jesus.

Judges 5: 31 is the closing line of Deborah's victory song, celebrating God's deliverance and the peace that followed bold leadership. That kind of peace doesn't come from playing it safe. It comes from trusting God enough to rise up, speak truth, and lead with love.

Leadership isn't always a title, it's an influence. Whether you're leading in your family, your community, your riding group, or your workplace, remember that real courage doesn't roar; it listens, prays, in acts with divine wisdom.

Reflection: Where is God calling you to lead right now?
How can you rely more on his wisdom than your own
strength as you step forward in courage?

Prayer: Heavenly Father, Thank you, for the courage you
give and the wisdom you freely offer.

Like Deborah, I want to lead in whatever space you place
me with boldness, clarity, and a heart that honors you.

Help me to rise like the sun in strength, reflecting your
light to the world.

Amen.

DATE

S M T W T F S

TAKE A MOMENT EACH DAY TO REFLECT ON THE THINGS
YOU'RE THANKFUL FOR

TODAY'S FOCUS

_____
_____
_____

TODAY I AM GRATEFUL FOR...

_____
_____
_____

SOMETHING THAT INSPIRED ME TODAY

PEOPLE I'M GRATEFUL TO HAVE
IN MY LIFE

Answered prayers

_____
_____
_____
_____
_____
_____

Notes & Free Thoughts

DAY 30 *scripture*

> Therefore, since we are surrounded by such a great cloud of witnesses, let us throw off everything that hinders and the sin that so easily entangles. And let us run with perseverance the race marked out for us, fixing our eyes on Jesus, the pioneer and perfector of faith.
>
> Hebrews 12:1-2

Faith on Two Wheels

Every ride starts with a decision to trust the road, the bike, and your ability to keep moving forward. Riding takes balance, awareness, and courage. And in many ways, so does walking out our faith.

Faith on two wheels isn't just about the physical ride-it's about the spiritual journey. It's choosing trust over fear, purpose over aimlessness, and Christ over comfort. It's knowing the road won't always be smooth, but God's presence will always be steady.

The writer of Hebrews calls us to run-or ride-with perseverance. That means keeping your hands on the handlebars of hope even when the terrain is rough. It means not riding alone, but recognizing the" great cloud of witnesses" cheering you on-those who've gone before, and sisters riding alongside you now.

As you come to the end of this devotional journey, know that this is just the beginning of the road ahead. Your faith is not confined to a quiet time or a journal-it rides with you in every mile, every challenge, and every triumph.

Keep your eyes on Jesus. Let your faith roar louder than your fears.

And ride on!

Reflection: Looking back over your faith journey, where have you seen God's hand the most clearly? How can you carry those moments forward as reminders of his faithfulness in every mile to come?

Prayer: Heavenly Father, Thank you for being my constant companion on this ride of life. Strengthen my faith for the road ahead.

Help me to ride with joy, courage and purpose.

Let my life be a testimony of your grace and power. May I always fix my eyes on you and never ride alone.

Amen.

DATE

S   M   T   W   T   F   S

TAKE A MOMENT EACH DAY TO REFLECT ON THE THINGS YOU'RE THANKFUL FOR

TODAY'S FOCUS

_____

_____

_____

TODAY I AM GRATEFUL FOR...

_____

_____

_____

SOMETHING THAT INSPIRED ME TODAY	PEOPLE I'M GRATEFUL TO HAVE IN MY LIFE

Answered prayers

_____

_____

_____

_____

_____

_____

Notes & Free Thoughts

Notes & Free Thoughts

_____
_____
_____
_____
_____
_____
_____
_____
_____
_____
_____
_____
_____
_____
_____
_____
_____
_____
_____
_____
_____

Notes & Free Thoughts

_____
_____
_____
_____
_____
_____
_____
_____
_____
_____
_____
_____
_____
_____
_____
_____
_____
_____

Notes & Free Thoughts

_____

_____

_____

_____

_____

_____

_____

_____

_____

_____

_____

_____

_____

_____

_____

_____

_____

♥

Notes & Free Thoughts

_____
_____
_____
_____
_____
_____
_____
_____
_____
_____
_____
_____
_____
_____
_____
_____
_____
_____
_____

♥

Notes & Free Thoughts

_____
_____
_____
_____
_____
_____
_____
_____
_____
_____
_____
_____
_____
_____
_____
_____
_____
_____
_____
_____

Notes & Free Thoughts

Notes & Free Thoughts

_____
_____
_____
_____
_____
_____
_____
_____
_____
_____
_____
_____
_____
_____
_____
_____
_____
_____
_____
_____

♥

Notes & Free Thoughts

Notes & Free Thoughts

_____
_____
_____
_____
_____
_____
_____
_____
_____
_____
_____
_____
_____
_____
_____
_____
_____
_____
_____
_____
_____
_____

♥

Notes & Free Thoughts

_____
_____
_____
_____
_____
_____
_____
_____
_____
_____
_____
_____
_____
_____
_____
_____
_____
_____
_____
_____
_____

Notes & Free Thoughts

_____

_____

_____

_____

_____

_____

_____

_____

_____

_____

_____

_____

_____

_____

_____

_____

_____

_____

♥

Notes & Free Thoughts

_____

_____

_____

_____

_____

_____

_____

_____

_____

_____

_____

_____

_____

_____

_____

_____

_____

♥

Notes & Free Thoughts

_____

_____

_____

_____

_____

_____

_____

_____

_____

_____

_____

_____

_____

_____

_____

_____

_____

_____

Notes & Free Thoughts

_____
_____
_____
_____
_____
_____
_____
_____
_____
_____
_____
_____
_____
_____
_____
_____
_____
_____
_____
_____
_____

Notes & Free Thoughts

_____
_____
_____
_____
_____
_____
_____
_____
_____
_____
_____
_____
_____
_____
_____
_____
_____
_____
_____
_____
_____
_____

Notes & Free Thoughts

_____
_____
_____
_____
_____
_____
_____
_____
_____
_____
_____
_____
_____
_____
_____
_____
_____
_____
_____
_____

Notes & Free Thoughts

Notes & Free Thoughts

_____
_____
_____
_____
_____
_____
_____
_____
_____
_____
_____
_____
_____
_____
_____
_____

Notes & Free Thoughts

_____
_____
_____
_____
_____
_____
_____
_____
_____
_____
_____
_____
_____
_____
_____
_____
_____

Notes & Free Thoughts

_____
_____
_____
_____
_____
_____
_____
_____
_____
_____
_____
_____
_____
_____
_____
_____
_____
_____
_____
_____

Notes & Free Thoughts

_____
_____
_____
_____
_____
_____
_____
_____
_____
_____
_____
_____
_____
_____
_____
_____
_____
_____
_____

Notes & Free Thoughts

Notes & Free Thoughts

_____
_____
_____
_____
_____
_____
_____
_____
_____
_____
_____
_____
_____
_____
_____
_____
_____
_____

Notes & Free Thoughts

Notes & Free Thoughts

_____
_____
_____
_____
_____
_____
_____
_____
_____
_____
_____
_____
_____
_____
_____
_____
_____
_____
_____

♥

Notes & Free Thoughts

_____

_____

_____

_____

_____

_____

_____

_____

_____

_____

_____

_____

_____

_____

_____

_____

_____

_____

_____

_____

Notes & Free Thoughts

_____

_____

_____

_____

_____

_____

_____

_____

_____

_____

_____

_____

_____

_____

_____

_____

_____

_____

_____

_____

_____

_____

Notes & Free Thoughts

_____

_____

_____

_____

_____

_____

_____

_____

_____

_____

_____

_____

_____

_____

_____

_____

_____

Notes & Free Thoughts

_____

_____

_____

_____

_____

_____

_____

_____

_____

_____

_____

_____

_____

_____

_____

_____

_____

Notes & Free Thoughts

Notes & Free Thoughts

_____
_____
_____
_____
_____
_____
_____
_____
_____
_____
_____
_____
_____
_____
_____
_____
_____
_____

Notes & Free Thoughts

Notes & Free Thoughts

_____
_____
_____
_____
_____
_____
_____
_____
_____
_____
_____
_____
_____
_____
_____
_____
_____
_____
_____
_____

Notes & Free Thoughts

_____
_____
_____
_____
_____
_____
_____
_____
_____
_____
_____
_____
_____
_____
_____
_____
_____
_____

♥

Notes & Free Thoughts

_____
_____
_____
_____
_____
_____
_____
_____
_____
_____
_____
_____
_____
_____
_____
_____
_____
_____
_____
_____
_____

Notes & Free Thoughts

_____
_____
_____
_____
_____
_____
_____
_____
_____
_____
_____
_____
_____
_____
_____
_____
_____

Notes & Free Thoughts

_____

_____

_____

_____

_____

_____

_____

_____

_____

_____

_____

_____

_____

_____

_____

_____

_____

_____

♥

Notes & Free Thoughts

_____

_____

_____

_____

_____

_____

_____

_____

_____

_____

_____

_____

_____

_____

_____

_____

_____

_____

_____

Notes & Free Thoughts

_____

_____

_____

_____

_____

_____

_____

_____

_____

_____

_____

_____

_____

_____

_____

_____

_____

_____

♥

Notes & Free Thoughts

_____

_____

_____

_____

_____

_____

_____

_____

_____

_____

_____

_____

_____

_____

_____

_____

_____

♥

Notes & Free Thoughts

_____
_____
_____
_____
_____
_____
_____
_____
_____
_____
_____
_____
_____
_____
_____
_____
_____
_____
_____
_____

♥

Notes & Free Thoughts

_____
_____
_____
_____
_____
_____
_____
_____
_____
_____
_____
_____
_____
_____
_____
_____
_____
_____
_____
_____

Notes & Free Thoughts

♥

Benediction

May the road rise to meet you,

May the wind of the spirit be always
at your back.

May your faith be bold, your heart at
peace, and your journey marked by
grace.

Ride with purpose.
Lead with courage.

Rest in His love.

And never forget-you never ride alone.

Thank you for purchasing this journal. Need to Reorder?

Want to see what else is new from me?

Check out my website here: